CW01430983

BE BETTER THAN BEFORE:

How to Become the Best Version of Yourself by Following an Easy Guide for Self-growth

STOSMO

ISBN: 9781705537879

information is without contract or any type of guarantee assurance.

DEDICATION

Dedicated to my mother Josiane, and my two brothers Dimitri and Pascal, the most motivational people I know.

CONTENTS

INTRODUCTION

I want to thank you and congratulate you for downloading the book, "Better than Before: How to become the best version of yourself by following an easy guide for self-growth."

This book contains proven steps and strategies on how to become a "best" version of yourself. You will learn all the valuable tools and strategies you need to help you evolve mentally, physically and emotionally. By using these tools consistently every day, you will soon discover their powerful effects and create a better version of yourself in every aspect of your life.

You will learn about:

Positive thinking – how being positive can make good things happen

Identifying your strengths and weaknesses – so you can utilise your strengths to their full advantage while improving on your weaknesses

Using empowering daily rituals – by setting daily rituals you can get more done

Time management – by planning your day, week, month you can prioritise urgent jobs and achieve things in the best order

Vision Boards – creating vision boards can help you to apply strong focus to your biggest goals

Daily goals – how setting daily goals can help you achieve more

Physical activity – fight anxiety, stress and depression naturally. Become healthier and happier

Healthy Eating – how healthy eating can literally change your life

Staying motivated – it can be hard to keep your mojo, so we will look at tips to help you

Being present – learn how to truly see what's in front of you

Love and gratitude – by practicing love and gratitude you will attract the same back to yourself

Self-reflection and spirituality – how reflecting on what you do and using spirituality can help you become better than before

These strategies can help you get the career you dream about, succeed in your relationships and find real self-fulfilment and happiness.

Thanks again for downloading this book, I hope you enjoy it!

1 THE POWER OF POSITIVE THINKING

It can be very easy to fall into the habit of finding fault with everything around you when life seems to be treating you unfairly. But, unfortunately, this negative behaviour will do only one thing, attract more pain and negativity toward you.

How do you view the world? Are you a natural pessimist or are you an optimist? Science has proven that by exercising your positivity you will allow positive things to happen. Pessimism is often a self-fulfilling prophecy, so beware to avoid pessimistic, cynical and negative behaviour.

It may seem like a simple thing to be optimistic, but the truth is that psychologically it is far more difficult for us to show feelings such as optimism, gratitude, joy, hope and contentment than it is for us to focus on negative emotions such as anger, disappointment, sadness or pain.

Consider how you deal with two situations and how long the feelings stay with you. If something wonderful happens to you or a loved one you feel joy, but that feeling is very short lived and quickly passes. If something bad happens, we hold it close for a great deal longer. Birth and death are a good example of this. If a loved one had a baby you would feel joy for them, but if that loved one died you would feel pain that would last far longer than the joy would have.

Neuroplasticity

This is the brain's ability to learn and grow. Much of this takes place in our prefrontal cortex, the part of our brain in our forehead, which develops when we have regular happy thoughts.Here our thoughts gather and are where our emotions from the deep limbic brain can be controlled. This allows us to focus and be aware of our thought processes resulting in reasoned thinking.

Negative thoughts and feelings reduce the metabolic energy normally given to the prefrontal cortex and prevents it from functioning correctly. Therefore, when you are stressed or afraid, it is difficult to think clearly.

Studies done using brain imaging technology have also demonstrated that negative thoughts also reduce the activity normally seen in the cerebellum. This is the part of the brain that controls the speed of our thoughts, along with balance and coordination.

The prefrontal cortex is where you decide how much attention should be paid to something, based upon how it makes you feel. The more focus is given to a negative thought, the more neural pathways are created to support that negative thought, which in turn affects other parts of our brain and our brain's ability to function. It essentially impedes cognition, speed of thought and reasoned thinking.

Not only does negative thinking stop the brain from working efficiently, but it has also been shown that it can have an effect on physical health too.

Negative thoughts can:

- Reduce your brain coordination
- Lower your creative abilities
- Make clear thinking and problem solving difficult
- Lower the activity in the cerebellum
- Trigger your left temporal lobe which controls fear, thus negatively affecting your mood, impulse control and memory

Positive thoughts can:

- Increase cognition and mental productivity
- Allow you to focus and pay attention
- Improve your ability to analyse information and solve problems quickly
- Create positive mental pathways that can form good habits

- Enhance creative thinking

As you can see, positive thinking makes our ability to function and use higher order thinking skills far greater. While we are being negative, our brains simply do not function well. If we want to perform at our best, we need to keep our thinking positive and our brain happy.

As an example, say you loved chocolate and thought that working a simple job in a chocolate factory would be fun – just think about all the free chocolate you could get. In the chocolate factory, you were responsible for watching the chocolates travel along a conveyor belt and you were tasked with checking that each and everyone was in perfect condition before entering the packaging area. It isn't easy to anticipate that over a relatively short period of time you would begin to despise that job for the monotony and boredom it caused you. But it would probably also have another effect. You may well find yourself also despising chocolates too. The mere sight or smell of chocolate would cause your brain to react like it does when you are depressed because it is strongly linked to the negative feelings produced by the job.

If you think about it, some people may cause you to feel down too. Do you know anyone who constantly moans and complains about everything? If you are in a great mood but are around that person for just a short time, can you literally feel your positive energy draining from you? Think about it the next time you see them.

Negativity is addictive, which is why being positive is so vitally important. We spend too much time thinking of all the bad things in our lives and hardly any focusing on the good. Be thankful for all the good things you do have in your life and stop focusing on the bad.

Not focusing on the bad doesn't mean you should just disregard your problems. What you should be doing instead of wallowing in them, is to find positive resolutions for them. There IS a positive resolution for every problem, no matter how large, you just need to go about finding it. If you can't do it alone then ask for expert advice. You will feel so much better once the problem is solved.

Remember that life isn't always easy, but it is a gift and we should be thankful and celebrate that.

2 IDENTIFYING STRENGTHS AND WEAKNESSES

Knowing what you are truly good at, and where you excel in life, as well as acknowledging areas where you could use a little help, can be really useful in not just your professional life but your personal one too. Understanding yourself at a deep level is a powerful tool that many people simply disregard. Just because you are not good at something does not make you a bad person or bad at your job and by admitting that you are not great and doing something about it this is far more positive and productive than simply pretending the problem does not exist. One thing is for sure. If you conquer the problem, it will never conquer you, but if you ignore it, it is bound to come and bite you on your behind.

To a greater extent, you will need to figure this out on your own, but there are ways to test your strengths and weaknesses and some tactics you can use to help you. First, test to see if your core values align with the life you are living. For example, perhaps you are passionate about the environment and reducing the toxic load on the planet. If you work in a factory that produces bottled water in plastic bottles this will be at odds with your core values and you won't feel truly happy in the job.

Another example could be that you have given up working to be a full-time stay at home parent because you think it is the right thing to do for your child. However, you feel fed up, frustrated and bored being at home all day and the parent-child groups don't help you much either because all you seem to talk about is each other's kids. You're desperate to get back to work where you can use your brain and have a grown-up conversation about something other than childhood ailments, pull-ups and the neighbour is 3-year-old who is still not talking. You may feel that going back to work full time would compromise your time with your child, so perhaps finding a balance and getting a part-time job or starting a home business could solve the problem so you can be part of both worlds.

Look hard at every aspect of your life, write down your perceived strengths and weaknesses in as many areas as you can:

- **Emotional** – are you strong minded or vulnerable ?

- **Character** – are you strong-willed and determined or are you shy and timid?

- **Physical** – Are you fit or unfit, strong, weak, etc.?

- **Qualifications** – What qualifications do you have, which qualifications do you need to get the career you want?

- **Experience** – What experience do you have, what experience do you need to get the job you most desire?

- **Skills** – What life skills and work skills do you have, which would be beneficial to improve your life and allow you to live the life of your dreams?

- **Money** – Are you good at making and saving money or do you spend every cent you have each month?

- **People & Relationships** – Are you good with people? Do you have a large circle of people you are friendly with, a close circle of very good friends, only a couple of friends or no friends at all? What are your people skills like? Do you make friends easily, or do you find it difficult – why? Are you in a long term, strong, healthy relationship or are you without a partner – why?

You may think of other areas of your life to explore along the way but starting with these will give you a good overview.

Once you have written down your strengths and weaknesses, make comments about them. Look at how you can further deepen and support your strengths and how you can overcome your weaknesses by turning them into strengths. Remember, some things you consider weaknesses could actually be strengths, it all depends on the situation.

If you have difficulty identifying your strengths and weaknesses in certain areas, then ask people to help you out. You can do a Reflective Best Self (RBS) exercise that can let you know what others think about your strengths. There is plenty of information on these exercises available on the internet. This type of exercise does not have to be limited to your friends but can include work colleagues, partners, family, old boss, teacher and so on. By asking people in different areas of your life to do this for you, you will get a better overview. Provide them with a way of answering the questions anonymously if you want to get truthful answers. If people know that you will know they gave the answers you may not always receive truthful results.

Once you receive the results look for recurring responses. This will allow you to discover things you may not even have considered when evaluating yourself. Don't look upon any negative responses as being bad, instead use them to improve yourself in that area.

3 EMPOWERING RITUALS

Most of us have some form of morning and evening rituals, and by rituals, I mean things that we do each and every day. In the morning we wash, brush our teeth and comb our hair and so on and similarly in the evening. Beyond this, meals form part of our daily rituals, but taking things beyond this and moving up to the next level can make a huge difference in our life, making it simpler and happier. Sound interesting? Let's find out some more.

Beyond the obvious, as I discussed above, it is important to think about how we, as a human being, function and the natural processes that occur in our body. Melatonin is the sleep hormone and it is released by our pineal gland in the brain as the light starts to diminish as the sun sets. The release of the hormone prepares our body for sleep and it is also a powerful antioxidant that supports and protects our immune system, reduces stress and aids the health of our nerves and body cells.

dressing emotional and psychological issues and taking time out for yourself are all ways to help improve your stress management.

2. **Diet**

An anti-inflammatory diet that reduces cortisol levels can be achieved by avoiding inflammatory foods, and ensuring you get enough nutrients:

- Avoid foods with a high glycemic load
- Avoid trans fats and saturated fats, but ensure you do consume the recommended level of Omega 3 fatty acids
- Reduce caffeine intake
- Do not consume alcohol in excess (see daily recommended guidelines)
- Insufficient consumption of foods rich in micronutrients and antioxidants – eat whole plant foods that are high in antioxidants and phytonutrients such as vegetables, fruits, whole grains, nuts, seeds and beans
- Eating insufficient fiber – eat high fiber foods such, many of which are the same as those in the point above

Cortisol is a necessary hormone that is important to our wellbeing when it exists in balance within the body, it is only when it remains in excess that problems develop. Melatonin is produced from Serotonin, our HAPPY hormone, and an imbalance in serotonin can result in insufficient melatonin levels. Everything is linked and maintaining balance is key.

Other rituals to add to your day:

Meditation
Eastern cultures have valued the art of meditation for 1000's of years and with good reason. Meditation can help both mind and body and has been proven to help many medical conditions.

By meditating as soon as you wake in the morning you can really kick-start your day. Try using affirmations and mantras to get your mindset positive. Similarly, meditate again before going to bed, this time try loving-kindness meditation to give thanks for your day.

Meditations don't need to be long and in fact, if you are new to meditating just 5 minutes is enough to start with. Then try to build up to between 15 and 30 minutes over time.

Stretching
If your life is spent sitting at a desk it is easy to become stiff and lose your natural suppleness. After you finish your meditation, spend just a few minutes doing simple body stretches to wake up the muscles and get the blood circulating. Doing this will help keep you supple; your muscles will be more relaxed, and it will help your body be prepared for the day.

Exercise

Once you've stretched, doing just 15 to 30 minutes of exercise that raises your heart rate and gets you moving can help you improve fitness, release "feel good" chemicals within your brain that lift your spirits and make you happy and prepared for the day ahead. Try not to do the same thing every day but mix it up a bit to keep things interesting. Exercise can be anything from a purposeful walk, jog or run to a short workout. There are 1000's of free short workout's available to watch and join in with online.

Get Outdoors
During the day try to spend some time outdoors. Exposure to sunlight or just natural light if it is cloudy can help support your natural sleep cycle as well as provide you with valuable vitamin D to support your immune system.

Breathing
If at any time of the day you find yourself feeling upset, anxious, cross or down, take a few minutes to do some breathing. This is simply placing all your concentration onto your breath. Breathe in deeply through your nose to the count of five. Now hold that breath to a further count of five and finally exhale through your mouth to the count of seven. If your mind wanders, simply bring it back to concentrating on your breathing and after just a few minutes you will find yourself feeling calm and back in control.

Doing this breathing exercise for a few minutes

right before you go to bed can help relieve stress and prepare you for sleep.

Things to Avoid!

Don't look at the media first thing in the morning as you want your day to start in as positive a way as possible and as the media typically reports mostly distressing stories it can affect your state of happiness. Don't read, watch or listen to anything that is not uplifting.

For several hours before bed avoid all stimulants, sugary foods and drinks, caffeine, nicotine and so on.

4 TIME MANAGEMENT

If you ever feel that there never seems to be enough hours in a day, then you are far from alone. By getting yourself truly organised you can manage your time more effectively and get a whole lot more done.

1. Daily Planning

Get yourself a planner so that each day you can turn the page and see the list of things that need doing. To keep on top of planning, allocate a small time slot each day when you can do it undisturbed. You can also review it and do some forward planning on your day off to make things quick and easy.

Complete your daily tasks in order of priority. Doing the washing, emptying the dishwasher, making the breakfast and so on. List them down and do them every day. On top of this, you then add tasks to the list that don't need doing daily, but that are more periodic such as cleaning the bathroom or vacuuming the living room. If you don't live alone, remember that you don't have to be the one to do all the tasks yourself, allocate people to do them. They live there too! Even small children can help with small tasks and the sooner they learn the more helpful they will be as they get older.

Now do the same at work, use a planner, either digital or paper to help you organise your week and your day. It will help you to keep on top of things. Make sure you do things in order of priority.

Prioritise wisely as follows:

- Urgent – Tasks that must be done immediately.
- Important – Tasks that are important but can wait a short while.
- Necessary – Tasks that are repetitive and require doing but are not urgent. When possible delegate these.
- Unimportant – Stuff that can really be done at any time by anyone. Again, delegate where possible.

Once you have prioritised tasks you will find your workload lightens considerably very quickly and will hopefully free time for you to do other things.

2. Stick with your Goals

Ensure that everything you do supports your goals, both short term and long term. Anything you do that does not support your goals is a waste of your time and should be cut out. This is true in all areas of your life, at home and at work.

3. Say "No"

Many of us seem to have difficulty using the word "no." The psychology behind this is that we don't like being told "no" ourselves, and it can make it difficult for us to say no to others when they make a request of us. If in your heart you don't want to do something, or you know it isn't as important as something else you need to do, then be kind to yourself and say "no."

4. Avoid Distractions

Note how many times a day someone distracts you when you are completing a task, both at home and at work. This can be someone physically distracting you by entering your office or it could be notifications on your computer or smartphone. Social media alerts can be a huge distraction and it can take great willpower to ignore them.

When you see how much time is wasted due to distractions you will soon realise that eliminating them is the best way to regain a lot of valuable time.

- Turn off all notifications on all devices
- Put your phone on silent and allow the answering service to take messages
- Put a sign on the door asking not to be disturbed unless absolutely necessary
- Ask your colleagues politely not to disturb you when working

Just taking a few simple steps like these will help you free time and help you feel less stressed. Constant disturbances destroy workflow, thought processes and creativity.

Set aside specific times of the day to catch up with email, phone messages and social media and stick to it.

5. Delegation

It can be difficult to let go of responsibilities but delegating to others will save you a lot of time and anxiety when things get tight. Get your kids and your partner to do things at home, create a tasks list for each of them and try rewarding kids when they do their tasks unprompted. In the workplace don't be afraid of asking colleagues for their help, supporting each other builds a stronger team.

6. Expenditure

One of the biggest stress factors in life is often money, or the lack of it to be precise. If you find your finances are often lacking just before payday then try tracking your expenditure more carefully and create a budget each month that you stick to. Tracking expenditure will help you to see where your money hemorrhages are and give you the chance to stop them. That way you can save money for when times are hard or for a special occasion. Having savings can be advantageous and save the day when something unexpected happens.

lected these images really narrow your focus and only select the ones that best represent what you really want. Then put them on your vision board like a collage of your ideas.

Some people choose to create their vision boards digitally but creating a physical vision board that you can touch, and feel is often more powerful at focusing your attention.

HOW VISUALISATION HELPS YOU ACHIEVE YOUR DESIRES:

The brain learns how to prepare our body to carry out actions. We imagine ourselves doing an activity and our brain runs through the process of doing it and then sends signals telling our body how to complete it.

Visualisation is a way of training your brain and your body to prepare to achieve your desires. By being open to your desires and allowing all the things you do to manifest the desired result, you achieve your dreams.

Consistency is important when you are acquiring a new skill or habit. Visualisation is a skill and should become a habit and daily repetition of your vision from looking at and thinking about your vision board can create strong, positive neural pathways in the brain that can help you achieve your goals.

It's no good putting your vision boards away in a cupboard or a draw, as they need to be placed where you can look at them as much as possible each and every day. Facing you on the wall in your office, on your fridge at home or wherever you will see them multiple times daily is the best bet.

Your boards only need to take up your time in their initial creation. After that, all you must do is look at them and allow your mind to think about the possibilities and be open to them.

MAKING YOUR VISION BOARD:

Vision boards are easy to make and fun. Before you start you should:

- **Prepare Your Space** – Find somewhere quiet where you can spread out your supplies and be left uninterrupted for a few hours.
- **Get Your Supplies** – Make sure you have everything you will need before you start. For a physical board, you will need the backing, which could be a piece of hardboard or strong cardboard. You will also need scissors or a craft knife, glue, and a printer if you are going to print images and this needs to be loaded with plenty of paper and ink, or other image materials such as magazines or photographs.
- **Set the Ambience** – It can be great to light some scented candles or use incense that is calming and comforting. Play relaxing music that helps to focus your concentration.
- **Boost Creativity** – To really get your creative juices flowing, try meditating before you begin to open your creative abilities and focus

your mind.

Once you are ready, you can start the creative process, here's how:

1. Plan Your Board

Think about the message you want your board to convey. What dreams and desires do you want to portray? Consider your key goals and values. If you are making a general life board think about your family, love life, health and wellbeing, hobbies and things you want to achieve.

2. Find Images

When you have a clear idea about what you want, start looking for images that best fit your desires.

3. Repeat

Repeat the process for each board that you want to make.

4. Centralise the Focus

Make sure that your biggest wish is placed centrally on the board and is a large clear image that draws your focus.

5. Consider Space

If you are limited for space, you may have to make smaller boards or make digital ones you can use as your screen savers or background on your phone or computer.

6. More Than Just Images

You don't only have to use images, you can also use quotes, objects, colour pallets and so on. For images, make sure they are of high quality and if you are creating a physical board ensure you stick them on well with a strong adhesive.

Once you have finished creating your boards place them where you will see them often each day. Allow yourself a few minutes each day to look at your board and allow positive thoughts it evokes to wash over you, renewing your energy and desire to achieve what you see.

Your vision board will not only remind you of what you most want in life, but it will also empower to you achieve your goals.

6 DAILY GOALS & MOTIVATION

By setting out your intentions for the day each morning and crossing each off as you achieve it, you will find this is highly rewarding and satisfying. Goals are slightly different to tasks in that tasks are jobs that must be done while goals are more than tasks and often require several tasks to be completed. They could be things like finishing all the arrangements for your partner's surprise birthday party or successfully completing all your coursework and so on.

The most successful people continually think about creating success. Your subconscious mind focuses on whatever it is you think about most often. If you are continually dwelling on your problems, then your mind will find more problems for you to think about. If you are thinking about solutions, achieving your goals and succeeding, then your subconscious mind will focus on these things instead.

Not only does your subconscious mind focus on your thoughts - be they positive or negative - but it also takes into account your emotions and listens to your feelings.

Positive thought is more than 100 times more powerful than negative thought and maintaining a positive mental attitude drives positive emotions into your subconscious.

If you find yourself getting caught up thinking about your problems, realign your focus to what you are doing and concentrate on getting things done. Think about your goals and achieving them. Never see your goals as chores, as they are positive achievements and reaching them should fill you with satisfaction and joy.

Setting Daily Goals

Let's look at how to set your daily goals:

1. You can have a goal book where you write down your goals of the day.

2. Make setting your goals one of the first things you do each day.

3. Set a deadline for reaching each one.

4. Don't get too ambitious as setting an unrealistic number of goals that you cannot manage will not be a positive experience.

5. Make sure you write down the goals in a positive way, don't let any negative words be used.

6. As you achieve a goal mark it off in your book.

By setting your goals like this each day, you are giving your creativity and motivation a jump start. Very quickly you will program yourself to focus on your goals and the best way to complete them.

You may make mistakes at first and find that some things are not as important as you thought they were, but quickly you will learn to order the goals in their level of importance.

Some goals will be recurring, while others will not. This will help you streamline your activities to achieve the recurring goals more quickly and efficiently.

Often you will notice that your goals change over time and different things start taking priority. Remember that you should have short- and long-term goals and although your long-term goals will take longer to reach, you should still focus on them each day and work towards achieving them.

Achieving Goals

Once you have set your goals you need to go about achieving them, here are some tips to help you succeed:

1. Be Realistic

If you set yourself unrealistic, or too many goals to achieve then you will defeat the purpose of goal setting. Goals must be achievable, but it does not mean they have to be easy. Completing challenging goals is far more rewarding than achieving simple ones.

2. Connections

Once you have set your goals, look for any connections between them. There are often connections between goals. For example, keeping fit and losing weight can be connected. When you have goals that share connections you can often combine your activities to achieve multiple things at once.

3. Set Different Objectives

It can be hard to stay focused on a long-term goal and maintain motivation to achieve it. To help with this, set shorter term objectives that take you ever closer to reaching your goal.

As an example, using the getting fit and losing weight example, your daily goals would be to do a certain amount of exercise and eat healthily, your weekly goals could be to have lost a certain amount of weight and run an extra two kilometres than you did the week before.

If your goal was to save a certain amount of money, then setting achievable monthly targets will help you reach your goal. If you wanted to save a little over $5,000 in the next six months, you know that each month you need to put aside $834 a month or $192 each week.

By breaking down your long-term goals into easier

bite-size chunks you are going to reach milestones quickly, which will maintain your motivation, and help you achieve what you want more easily.

4. Goal Review

Your daily goals can be marked off during the day as you achieve them, but weekly, monthly or longer-term goals should only be visited once a week when you have time to analyse your progress fully.

Look at what you have accomplished during the week and how well you are doing with reaching your longer-term goals. There will be times when you don't succeed in achieving a goal by the deadline you set for it. Rather than looking upon this negatively, look at why that happened and reset the goal making sure you take into account this time any issues you encountered previously. Goals are a great method of learning and learning should always be viewed as positive. We learn by our mistakes, so mistakes are also positive and just a necessary part of our daily life. Goal review should not take you long, just 15 to 20 minutes.

5. Give Your Goals Purpose

Set goals that have a strong purpose. Understand why you want to achieve each one of your goals as this gives it a reason for doing.

Make sure that your goals are your own and you want to achieve them for yourself and not because someone else has said it would be a good idea. It's fine to use suggestions from others, but the incentive must come from you. If a goal doesn't fulfill a purpose and have a reason that you want to achieve for yourself, then it isn't a goal worth pursuing.

Continual daily evaluation can seem like a chore and end up having a negative rather than a positive result. Here are some ways to help make self-evaluation a valuable and positive tool rather than a negative chore.

1. Set realistic goals - When doing your morning meditation take just a few moments to think about what you would like to realistically achieve by the end of the day. Then, in the evening, again think back to your thought of the morning and ask yourself simply "Did I achieve what I wanted?" and "Was my day a success?" If you can answer yes, then you know you have succeeded. If not, consider why you were unable to complete your goals and how you could be more successful in doing so in the future.

2. **Use tools to help you** – There are many different online apps and downloads that can help you stay on top of your goals and evaluate your progress for you in simple easy to use ways. Apps such as Nozebe, GoalsOnTrack, LifeTick, Strides, Coach.Me, Habit List, Irunurun and ActionAlly. Many offer free trials so you can road test them and see which work best for you.

3. **Stop procrastinating** – We often put off doing tasks that we are not looking forward to. The prob-

lem is by doing this they remain a constant nagging worry in our mind that can build up to be more than uncomfortable over time. Rather than putting off these tasks, learn to face them head on and rather than shoving them to the bottom of your priority list, bring them to the top and get them out of the way. It makes for a happier, lighter life.

Goal setting and goal achieving can really give your life meaning and purpose. You feel like you are succeeding as you can see real tangible results to your efforts. Goals can be set in all areas of your life, not just at work or at home. Make different goals so that all aspects of your life are benefitting from the power of achievement.

Motivation:

When you are consistently working towards achieving goals, particularly long-term ones, it can be easy to lose motivation. Your goal can often seem so far off that you think you might never get there.

New Year's resolutions are a good example of goals that many of us fail to meet. Only 20% of people who set New Year's resolutions actually achieve them, meaning a massive 80% will fail.

So how can you avoid falling foul of this problem and maintain your motivation and ensure you do achieve your goals?

1. **Chose goals that really matter**. If you are not passionate about achieving a goal you have set, then the likelihood is that you won't achieve it. Look at all aspects of your life career, relationships, family, friends, health and wellness, passions, environment and finances. Which of the areas are you the least happy with? And what do you want to change about them? Once you have worked out the what, you can work out the how. Set out a definitive plan with timescales to improve your chance of success.

2. **Ignore "I should…"** If you think "I should do X because my Mom really wants me to" for example, then you have lost before you even start. To maintain motivation, you need to be truly passionate about it for yourself and not for someone else.

3. **Break it down**. Long term goals can seem impossible and it is easy to lose motivation to achieve them. Break them down into a series of much smaller, simpler goals that will eventually lead you to reach success with your main objective. By doing this you are rewarding yourself each time you successfully complete a task that brings you another step closer.

4. **Competitiveness**. If your goal is to do something that someone else, you know also wants to achieve use this to provide some fun competitiveness. Competition is a great way to stay motivated and doing things with someone else rather than on your own can make it feel a lot easier.

7 PHYSICAL ACTIVITY

We all know that exercise is an essential element to our overall health and wellbeing. But far fewer people realise that it is also a profoundly important aspect to maintain good mental health too.

Regular exercise reduces stress, improves brain function and boosts memory, it aids restful sleep and improves your mood. Research has shown that just a modest amount of daily exercise can make a dramatic difference and it does not matter what your fitness level is, or your age or ability. Anyone can do some form of physical activity each day.

Mental Health Benefits

Although it would come as no surprise that exercise can help physical health, mental health benefits are just as apparent.

People who exercise regularly soon find that exercise gives them an all over sense of well-being. They have more energy, can think better, sleep more soundly and generally feel happier about themselves and their lives.

Most of us feel the effects of stress or anxiety from time to time. Exercise is a great way to help you conquer this as it relieves tension and enhances your feelings of well-being through the release of endorphins in the brain, which naturally make you feel good. If you use mindfulness when you are exercising, so notice everything around you, the sun on your face, wind in your hair, the feeling of your feet hitting the ground and so on, you will really focus your body and help you improve your condition faster. It also helps to stem the flow of worries that may otherwise plague your mind.

Exercise is also beneficial for people with mild depression and is as effective as antidepressant medication in some instances. By setting a regular exercise schedule you can help to prevent relapse too.

The reason why exercise fights depression so well is because it reduces inflammation, stimulates neural growth and sets new neural pathways that are linked to feelings of wellbeing. The release of endorphins generated during exercise keeps you feeling positive and help break negative thought patterns.

Because exercise also releases dopamine, norepinephrine and serotonin all brain chemicals that boost mood, memory, motivation and concentration it can also benefit people with ADHD Attention Deficit Hyperactivity Disorder or PTSD Post Traumatic Stress Disorder.

Mental Benefits of Exercise:

- **Better memory and sharper thinking** – this is caused by the same endorphins that help you feel good after exercise. They stimulate brain cells and can help your neuroplasticity as well as help age-related mental decline.
- **Heightened self-esteem** – Once regular exercise becomes a habit you will feel better about your appearance, creating an increased sense of self-worth, strength and resilience.
- **Higher energy levels** – Strengthening your body with exercise, increasing your heart rate and improving your fitness levels will result in you having more energy and more get up and go.
- **Improved sleep** – Exercise helps regulate sleep patterns. When used in conjunction with light therapy it can dramatically improve your quality of sleep.
- **Resilience** – Rather than turning to artificial aids to help deal with life's challenges such as alcohol or drugs, negative behaviors such as this can be more easily eliminated when you exercise regularly because you won't need the artificial aids to help you anymore.
- **Immune system** – Your immune system is strengthened with regular exercise as one of the main causes for a suppressed immune system, stress will be reduced.

More Is not Better

Scientists have discovered that there is no additional benefit to doing more than 30 minutes of exercise per day.

It could be that to start with you may even struggle with just doing 30 minutes, but don't worry, you don't need to start off at 30 minutes. Make it one of your goals to reach 30 minutes and build up to it over time.

Which Exercise is best?

There is no form of exercise better than another. More benefit is gained by cross training, this is doing more than one type of exercise so that your body is worked in different ways. For example, you could swim one day, walk or run the next, do an exercise class the day after that and so on. Mixing things up will keep your exercise interesting and working out a weekly exercise plan that works for you and fits well around your other commitments is the best solution if you are to make it habitual.

Some people find that they cannot manage to fit in a 30-minute exercise period on some days, but they may be able to fit in two 15-minute sessions instead. Don't give excuses for not doing exercise, make it work for you. If you really can't manage to exercise on workdays, then make a really big effort on your days off. You will gain almost as much benefit.

Benefit Level

You don't have to go crazy to get good results. Research has shown that just moderate exertion is enough to reap rewards. The exercise you do should make you breathe a little more heavily than normal, not make you completely out of breath. You should become warm, but you don't need to work yourself up into a lather of sweat.

Mental Barriers

Hopefully, you have found comfort in discovering that you don't need to do as much exercise or make it as exhausting as you may have previously thought in order to help your health. But when you are already tired or feeling down it can still be hard to make the effort to exercise.

If you're tired or stressed, you will find that by doing some exercise will energize you and make you feel a lot better. Focus on the fact that how you feel will be improved once you have exercised and you should be able to muster the willpower to do it. You'll be thanking yourself after.

Another barrier can be poor self-image. You don't want anyone to see you exercising! It does not matter how big you are or how unfit, you can start doing exercise in your own home or just going for a purposeful walk to start with. There will be beginners' classes for many fitness activities and you'll soon see that you are not alone, other people, just like you, will be there.

Pain is a powerful mental barrier. If you suffer from a disability or any kind it can seem difficult to find an exercise that is suitable for you. Often water-based exercise can be a good solution to the problem, or you can do fitness classes specially designed for people who are confined to sitting. Take a look online.

It is always advisable to discuss the best kind of fitness regime for you with your doctor or health care professional.

Once you have been doing your exercise for several weeks you will start noticing positive changes in your appearance, your fitness levels and in the way, you are feeling generally. All your hard work will be worth it.

8 HEALTHY EATING

Along with exercise, you have got to eat healthily to make a massive impact on your life. Eating healthy food that benefits your body will nourish not just your flesh but your mind and your soul.

Science is continually showing us that what we eat can both cause and prevent all manner of health issues and be the difference between living a long, healthy happy life and a short miserable pain filled one.

Make sure that everything you put into your mouth has value for your health.

If you are overweight, understand one simple fact. Dieting does not work! It never has and it never will. It does not work because you can't maintain a diet for your entire life. What does work is changing your eating habits permanently. Exchanging unhealthy foods for healthy ones and only eating what you need to eat to sustain you.

Healthy eating does not involve any strict dietary

limitations. You don't have to count calories or cut out any food groups. Healthy eating is about making better choices about what you eat and choosing foods that have benefits over those that are simply empty calories that can actually damage your long-term health.

Healthy Eating Fundamentals

Foods that are beneficial for the human body are those that have been subjected to no, or very limited processing. Many of the unhealthy foods we eat have their alternatives and for much of the time, it is simply a matter of exchanging the bad for the good. Unprocessed foods are called natural or whole foods and eating them can make big changes to the way you look and feel.

Balance has always been and always will be the cornerstone of a healthy diet. We need to eat foods from all the different food groups in order to maintain the best health.

There is quite a bit of controversy surrounding animal products, but quality here is key. Processed meats are bad for your health, while grass-fed unprocessed meats offer a lot of good health benefits:

You need to find sources of vitamin B12, which is needed by the body to maintain healthy nerves and blood cells. It also forms part of your body's DNA - the genetic material presents in all your cells. Vitamin B12 also helps in the prevention of megaloblastic anaemia that can make you weak and tired.

Vitamin B12 is ONLY found in animal products and cannot be found in plants.

Omega 3 fatty acids. Animal sources of Omega 3 are in a form called DHA, which is readily absorbed by the body. Plant-based sources of Omega 3 are in the form ALA, which the body cannot readily absorb.

Iron. The form found mostly in vegetables is called non-heme iron, which the body cannot be easily absorbed. Iron found in animal products is readily absorbable by the body.

Some essential nutrients are only found in animal products, particularly meat. This includes:

- Creatine – used for energy reserves in the muscles and brain.
- Carnosine – an antioxidant that prevents inflammation and removes free radicals from the body.

Rather than eliminating entire food groups as some diets suggest, what is needed is to select the healthiest foods in each food group.

Protein

Required for repair and growth. Protein provides energy and supports cognitive function and mood.

Protein can be from a plant-based source and can be found in quinoa, hemp seeds, chia seeds, broccoli, legumes (lentils, peas, beans, chickpeas), leafy greens, nuts and plant-based milk (soy, almond, hemp, rice) for example. Or an animal-based source such as meat, fish, eggs, and dairy products.

Fat

Fat is an essential part of a healthy diet because many vitamins are only fat soluble, so without fat, we would not be able to absorb and use them in our body. Fat is also necessary to build cell membranes and is essential in blood clotting and muscle movement. It helps prevent inflammation and improves our brain function, it provides us with energy and aids in stabilising our mood.

Not all fats are the same however, industrially manufactured fats like almost all other foods that undergo any form of processing or manufacture are bad for our health, while natural fats are generally good.

Good fats are found mostly in vegetables, nuts, seeds, and fish. Healthy fats are in liquid form at room temperature and are generally either known as monounsaturated or polyunsaturated.

1. Trans fats. These are a byproduct of a manufacturing process known as hydrogenation where healthy oils are converted to solids to prolong shelf life. Trans fats are bad news for our health, they have zero nutritional value and have been linked to cancer, heart disease, stroke, diabetes and other illnesses. Trans fats have been shown to increase harmful LDL cholesterol levels in the blood. No level of consumption of trans fats is considered to be safe.

2. Monounsaturated fats. These include olive oil, avocados, most nuts and peanut oil, safflower and sunflower oils. The Mediterranean diet, which is the foods eaten by people living on the Mediterranean coast is high in olive oil, fish and vegetables, and has been found to be very beneficial to health.

There is not a recommended daily amount for monounsaturated fats, but it is recommended that you use them to replace saturated and trans fats wherever possible.

3. Polyunsaturated Fats. These include corn oil, sunflower oil and safflower oil. Omega 3 and omega 6 fatty acids are polyunsaturated fats. They are called essential fats because they are necessary for the body to function normally.

Using these types of fats in your diet can help lower harmful LDL cholesterol and triglycerides.

Omega 3 is one of the most important fats to be included in the diet. Omega 3 can be found in fatty fish (mackerel, sardines and salmon) walnuts, flaxseeds, canola oil and un-hydrogenated soybean oil. Omega 3 oils have a broad range of health benefits and are especially beneficial to brain function.

Omega 6 fatty acids must be kept in balance with Omega-3's and are beneficial against heart disease. They can be found in vegetable oils including sunflower, safflower, walnut, corn and soybean.

4. Saturated fats. These come from animal and

vegetable sources and include fat found in red meat, dairy foods including cheese, coconut oil and many commercially produced baked goods and foods.

If your diet is high in saturated fats it can cause a rise in cholesterol that can be more detrimental to health, as it can block the arteries for this reason saturated fats are recommended to be kept to only a small portion of your food intake per day and should only account for about 10% of the calories you ingest.

The harm done by eating saturated fats can be increased or decreased depending on what else your diet contains. If you eat lots of healthy fiber-rich, low sugar food (vegetables, nuts, seeds, fruits and whole grains) then this can negate the effects of saturated fats to some degree. If however, your diet is high in saturated fats, sugar and processed carbohydrates (white bread, pasta, rice), then the dangers are a lot higher.

Fiber

High fiber foods lower your risk of heart disease, stroke and diabetes. They also maintain a healthy digestive system, can improve your skin and help you to reduce and maintain a healthy body weight.

Fiber-rich foods include whole grains, fruits, vegetables, nuts, seeds and beans.

Carbohydrates

One of the body's principal energy sources, carbohydrates should be eaten in their complex unrefined forms such as vegetables, whole grains, fruit and not refined carbohydrates such as white bread, pasta or rice, which turn almost instantly to glucose (sugar) in your body.

Eating healthy complex unrefined carbs will keep your energy levels balanced, avoid sugar spikes that can over time lead to insulin resistance, diabetes, food cravings and hormonal imbalance. Refined carbs can also affect your memory, mood, energy levels and cause your body to store the excess sugar into fat, increasing your waistline.

Stick with whole grains, unprocessed, unrefined, pure natural foods for top health.

Vitamins and Minerals

Vitamins and minerals are essential to good health, they help every process in the body and are found mainly in vegetables, fruits and animal products. Again, stay with the natural unrefined, unprocessed kind.

Dairy Products

Many people have intolerances to dairy products. This can be for several reasons and is often because we are human beings, not cows, so eating products made with cows 'milk is incompatible to the human organism. We are often allergic to the lactose in cows 'milk or the protein.

Another problem with dairy products is that any

that are not organically produced contain chemicals, antibiotics and other toxins given to the cows and transmitted through their milk.

Dairy products are not essential in our diet, but they are a good source of calcium and vitamin D. If you cannot, or do not want to, consume dairy products ensure that you are getting enough calcium from other sources such as seeds, spinach, black-eyed peas, beans, lentils, almonds, okra, oily fish (sardines, trout, salmon, mackerel), acorn squash, clams.

Switching to a Healthy Diet

It is best to make the change to a healthy diet gradually. Start by cutting out the worst foods for you that are high in a combination of sugar and fat. Exchange your processed carbohydrates such as white bread, white pasta and white rice for their whole grain versions. Reduce the amount of sugar you eat by making your own cakes, biscuits and sweets and use natural sugar alternatives monk fruit, bacon syrup, stevia and NON-GMO erythritol. A neat trick is using ripe bananas in chocolate cakes instead of sugar.

Be sure you completely avoid any foods or drinks with artificial sweeteners (check the labels!) such as aspartame and saccharin – this stuff is linked with serious health problems and should never be consumed.

Stop buying food that is contaminated with pesticides and herbicides and buy organic. Yes, it costs a little more, but the benefits to your health are worth every cent. Even better grown your own!

Processed meals are seriously bad news. Yes, they may be convenient, but they contain all kinds of preservatives and additives you would not need your dog, so why on earth would you give them to yourself and your kids?! If you need quick easy meals during your busy working week then cook up a few batches of tasty nutritious meals on your day off. If you are clever you can make tasty nutritious food in big batches to keep in your freezer in hand portion-sized containers. Chili con-carnie, bolognese sauce, curry, tagine and so on are easy one-pot dishes you can whip up in large batches in no time.

Don't completely exclude treats, change them. Ice cream made with almond milk sweetened with raw honey is totally delicious. Dark chocolate has lots of health benefits and once you are accustomed to it, you will wonder why you ever liked milk chocolate. Think laterally and look on the internet for great tasting healthy recipe ideas.

9 MINDFULNESS, GRATITUDE AND LEARNING TO LOVE YOURSELF

Three things that can really help you achieve inner peace and happiness are mindfulness, gratitude and loving yourself. Here we will look at these three elements in isolation to learn how.

Mindfulness

Mindfulness, or being present, helps you see the world fully and clearly. It can help you when you are feeling uncertain, fearful, angry or resentful and helps you to work through it mindfully.

Being present is about living your life in the moment and not dwelling on the past of worrying about the future. Living your life in the here and now essentially eliminates huge amounts of stress and worry.

It sounds great, but it can be quite hard to achieve,

especially when you are not used to doing it. Here are a few ways to help you:

- Using meditation. As we have discussed elsewhere in the book, meditation is a great tool for helping you live a life with less stress. When you are meditating you should be using mindfulness and being present as part of your meditation. Your mind is in the here and now although you still pay it no attention.

- Reminders. Because it is easy to forget to be mindful and present when you first start, try setting reminders to bring your attention back to what is happening now. You can do this by setting regular alarms on your phone, or by using apps that are designed to help you with this. You can also train your mind by setting reminders using physical things such as objects in your room. Every time you glance at them, they remind you to be mindful.

Gratitude

Being grateful helps you to experience the world in a positive way. It can make you feel more alive, help you to be more compassionate and kinder and even strengthen your immune system and improve your sleep.

Gratitude does not need to be reserved for "special events" such as promotions or passing exams. Gratitude should be practiced for all manner of things, from the smallest kindness that someone shows you to the meals you eat each and every day.

Be thankful for new things each and every day. When you review your day think about what was great about it and be thankful for it. When you meditate, practicing some loving kindness meditations can really help you ramp up your gratitude levels.

You can be grateful for all kinds of things; someone doing you a favor, or just for having a family who loves you. Try and think about specifics, so if your partner made you a special meal or even just gave you a peck on the cheek before you left for work, be grateful for it.

Open your eyes and see what the world is giving you. Before long you will be noticing more and more each day and this constant stream of good things will, in turn, manifest more good things and your happiness and contentment will benefit significantly.

Love Yourself

You may well have heard that you need to love yourself before you can love anyone else. This can be hard to achieve because most of us are in some way insecure about ourselves, our weight, skin, face, voice, hair, etc. There is a ton of reasons that we find not to like about ourselves, let alone love.

The truth is that sometimes the only way to learn to love yourself is to be loved regardless of our insecurities. This is not so simple, however, as our insecurities can stop us connecting deeply with another person or if someone is derisive about us in some way, our vulnerability and self-consciousness is increased even more.

It is common for us to hide our true self from others and instead to invent a persona, a character that we show to the world. Often this character will openly admit their faults to others and even laugh at them, which is clearly rather self-destructive but is something we use as a coping mechanism because it is less painful to do this to ourselves than have someone else do it to you.

Imagine this – you have met someone you really, *really* like but have felt the pain of rejection too many times to even try and connect with them. It is rather like putting a dog into a yard with an electric fence they cannot see. Each time they try to leave the yard they get zapped by the fence and quickly learn that they must stay within its confines. A meaty bone is placed just outside of the fence (like the person you like), but the dog is still too scared to try and pass the fence even if it is starving. When pushed to go toward the bone it will display anxiety and fear because to it, getting that bone simply isn't worth the pain it would suffer getting there.

Even if you turned the fence off, the animal would still be too afraid to go past that invisible boundary and it has been programmed to expect to be zapped. If after a long while it finally finds the courage to cross that line it will be filled with fear and mental anguish expecting that painful shock to happen at any moment.

This is no different with us, showing our true self, our deepest emotions are too scary, our instincts tell us not to try because we will only get hurt again.

We learn to do this from an early age and by the time we reach adulthood most of us have mastered it. Think about it, is the "you" you show the world the real you?

Finding your way back to you and having the strength to show that person and share them with the world can be tough. But if you are going to find real happiness and love, which must be based on honesty and trust, then it must be done. Look around you at people in your life that you feel you could trust to show the real you. Try it out a few times and don't be afraid. Even if you do get a negative response, don't blame yourself for it. It is not your fault but almost certainly theirs. You will find people who you can be your true self around, and they will become your real friends. It is from these people you are most likely to find your life partner and the path back to loving yourself for who you are and not who others want you to be.

Printed in Great Britain
by Amazon